The Best 100 Songs That You Never Heard

JEFFREY BRIAN ROMEO

authorHOUSE®

AuthorHouse™
1663 Liberty Drive
Bloomington, IN 47403
www.authorhouse.com
Phone: 833-262-8899

Published by AuthorHouse 06/28/2023

ISBN: 979-8-8230-1085-6 (sc)
ISBN: 979-8-8230-1087-0 (e)

Library of Congress Control Number: 2023911582

Print information available on the last page.

Any people depicted in stock imagery provided by Getty Images are models,
and such images are being used for illustrative purposes only.
Certain stock imagery © Getty Images.

This book is printed on acid-free paper.

Because of the dynamic nature of the Internet, any web addresses or
links contained in this book may have changed since publication and may
no longer be valid. The views expressed in this work are solely those
of the author and do not necessarily reflect the views of the publisher,
and the publisher hereby disclaims any responsibility for them.

Contents

Preface

Growing up in West Virginia, going to school, going to concerts, playing sports, making lifelong friends and pals, music and song lyrics was always a fascination of mine and now looking back, it reminds me of certain chapters in my life.

I really have no musical talent, but I truly appreciate talented people and their music. I grew up with several buddies that could sing and play, and some still do. I feel like I know music very well but I'm just not very good at singing and playing it for some reason. Growing up, it seemed like I was the one that often discovered great music before others, at least in my stomping grounds. Most of my friends often admired my music collection even though some never even heard of some of my bands. I was not in to the top 40.

My first love was hard rock and heavy metal but then I found classic and southern rock, alternative and country. My sister was a dead head, so I found her records and even liked hippy music. More recently, I started liking the sounds of gospel and bluegrass. But with all that said, it was the lyrics that fascinated me. I was the kid that opened the album or CD cover to read the lyrics. I read some of the most beautiful lyrics and some of the most darkest and evil lyrics and I loved it. You would not catch me reading many books but reading the lyrics, now that was cool. I used to draw pictures and write them all over my high school book covers.

I really cannot list all my influences, but my favorites would be bands like Guns N Roses, Zakk Wylde, Alice in Chains, Metallica, Pantera, Megadeth, Ozzy, Black Sabbath, Iron Maiden, Dio, Ratt, Motley Crue, Judas Priest, KISS, AC/DC, Cinderella, WASP, Stryper, Junkyard, Queen, Rolling Stones, Tony Carey, Hank Williams Jr, David Allan Coe, Johnny Cash, Elvis, Willie Nelson, Jamey Johnson, Toby Keith, Lynyrd Skynyrd, Kings X, Soundgarden, Stone Temple Pilots, Nirvana, Janes Addiction, Mother Love Bone, Rage Against the Machine, The Cult, Faith No More, Rancid, Eric Johnson, Simon and Garfunkel, Creedence Clearwater, Eagles, Bon Jovi, Jack Johnson, Ugly Kid Joe, Anthrax, Jackyl, Danzig, Slayer and so on. I could listen to Stick Figure, Sturgill Simpson, Led Zeppelin and Motorhead in the same car ride, and many more.

I wrote some things when I was in college but never with any music background. During Covid, I picked up the guitar and taught myself some basic chords and then started humming out lyrics and I was hooked. I didn't know it would turn into this but after a while, the words just started popping out. I wanted to write about a variety of subjects and try to change up my style as much as possible so it would not be predictable. Well, as you read, some of it is predictable and follows a pattern but that is because I have musical limitations.

Not to scare you, but I wrote about everything, not all of it is true, some songs are 100% true, some are 50% true, some are enhanced to draw attention or simply to rhyme, and some songs are total fiction. You can figure it out for yourself. Some people will read one song and recognize everything in it as a true story that they remember, and other songs people will be like- dang he is mentally disturbed- LOL. I wrote about growing up in WV, family, friends, animals, holidays, college life, drinking, drugs, fighting, life and death, heaven, girls, politics, pretty things, ugly things, and even some sci fi. Some of the lyrics may be raunchy and some may make you laugh, and some may make you cry.

This is a collection of works that contain a few songs and poems that I wrote in college, but most were written between 2020 and 2023. Most of them have chords and riffs to them but they are very basic so I am hoping someday, someone famous will ask me to hear it or maybe even make it their own.

4th of July

I'm a drinking and a fishing down at the lake
I can't catch a thing and it's getting late
It's time to pack it up and get on back

She's waiting and thinking and getting loud
On the front porch of her grandma's house
Where the flag flies high on the 4th of July

You can see the heat coming from her eyes
And feel the tension a mile wide
Trying to survive on the 4th of July

Her daddy said boy don't you leave
It's best to beg down on your knees
Than to face that dynamite on the 4th of July

We rode horses on my buddy's farm
And we drank all night in his uncle's barn
Invited a few more friends and we got down

It was Jim Beam whiskey and playing cards
Blasting GNR out in the yard
We got high on the 4th of July

You can feel the pride in a double wide
And see the lights all over the sky
It's a hell of a night on the 4th of July

We never forget what it's all about
The battles we won and lost throughout
In the smoke and fire on the 4th of July

I ran away from home once or twice
But I always came back with my appetite
Momma I was such a stupid kid

We met girls at the Varsity Club
We drank beer at the local pubs
Spent my dime on the 4th of July

Times like this bring the best of it
Family first is the way we live
Our flag flies high on the 4th of July

Times like this bring the best of it
Country proud is the way we live
Our flag flies high on the 4th of July

Times like this bring the best of it
America first is the way we live
Our flag flies high on the 4th of July

21 to 69

I aint no Wilt Chamberlain and I aint Gene Simmons
But I slay the ***** like it's my religion
I aint no Tiger Woods and I aint Jack Nicholas
But I put it in the hole like I'm making a living

Some say sex is overrated but those who don't get more creative
From 21 to 69
Some things get better as we age like wine and women and
my dating range
From 21 to 69

I aint no Tom Brady and I aint Joe Namath
But I score with the ladies almost every minute
I aint no Donald Trump and I aint Bill Clinton
But I'm better looking in own my opinion

Some say sex is overrated but those who don't get more creative
From 21 to 69
Some things get better as we age like wine and women and
my dating range
From 21 to 69

A Better Life

I'm from the hills and the mines and I graduated from the bottom of my class
But I made my way, made my pay and I didn't end up dead last
I pushed forward and I pushed back, and I found my lucky path
I paid my dues and surprised a few that I made it past
I made it past the deadly traps, the traps that catch us all
I made it past the deadly traps and the concrete blocks in the wall

Take the bricks and take your licks and take them one by one
Take the chance and follow the light that leads you to a better life

I'm from the north and I moved down south to start my life and career
But my admiration and satisfaction slid into a trench and began to disappear
I jumped up and down and I jumped thru my share of hoops
I lost friends and wore out my welcome and I put on my cowboy boots
My boots that were made for walking, walking down the hall
My boots that were made for walking and running from the law

Take the bricks and take your licks and take them one by one
Take the chance and follow the light that leads you to a better life

A Dog Will Always Stray

Life was good when our time began
But if it was up to you, I'd never see my friends
I remember when you used to beg to stay
You laid in bed but then you ran away

Wet hair bad breath was just a clue
She made her name in town running loose

Chewed up my brand new shoes
Peed in my living room
She is my living proof
That a dog will always stray

Chased down the man next door
Crapped on my kitchen floor
You proved to me once more
That a dog will always stray

One hour feels like a day
One day feels like a week away
I miss my brat and I miss my pet
Remember when she used to lick my neck

I pumped the brakes on a straightaway
I closed my eyes and began to pray

Chewed up my brand new shoes
Peed in my living room
She is my living proof
That a dog will always stray

Chased down the man next door
Crapped on my kitchen floor
You proved to me once more
That a dog will always stray

A Yesterday That Aint Worth All The Words

I was working late from noon til eight
And I got home just past nine
I couldn't believe I was so naïve
That I didn't see the signs

I traveled abroad and I studied law
But I got out thought by a fool
I'll never surrender, and I'll never forgive her
For being so mean and cruel

Yesterday it hurt me but today it's behind me
I know my values and my worth
It was just another day it was just a yesterday
That aint worth all the words

I sat on my back porch after my divorce
And cussed into the sky
My dog ran away my cat was a stray
And my goldfish just died

It wasn't a good day my hair turned gray
And I gained another pound
My wife couldn't stand me she was always angry
So, she didn't stick around

Yesterday it hurt me but today it's behind me
I know my values and my worth
It was just another day it was just a yesterday
That aint worth all the words

Absolute Prostitute

I see the way you look
You look at me I shook
I can't believe it took

All of the smoke and drugs
All of the charm and tugs
To get your clothes undone

I am the absolute – I never tell
the truth
I eat the passion fruit- all thru
the night
I am a prostitute- I never let
you loose
You play the simple fool- all
of your life

I will take all of you
You will become subdued
You will not make it thru

All of the ups and downs
All of the ins and outs
Will make your mom so proud

I am the absolute – I never tell the truth
I eat the passion fruit- all thru the night
I am a prostitute- I never let you loose
You play the simple fool- all of your life

Act Like You Been There Before

You got nothing but it's adding up fast
You got to make it count
You fly low but there's no where to go
You got to let your wheels down
You need to open your eyes to see
What life's all about

Place all your chips on a pair of queens
When the dealer shows nineteen
Something new is something great
Act like you been there before babe- you got to

Act like you been there before and the world belongs to you
Act like you been there before and there's nothing you can't do
Act like you been there before when you walk right thru the door

She keeps comin like a train on the tracks
She's gonna wreck your mind
Deep down in the depths of hell
You got to dig your way out
You dream about all the things you want
You got to wake up now

I had my first shot of old Jim Beam
At the age of seventeen
Something new is something great
Act like you been there before babe- you got to

Act like you been there before and the world belongs to you
Act like you been there before and there's nothing you can't do
Act like you been there before when you walk right thru the door

Alabama Original

If I woke up tomorrow in another dream
It wouldn't be any better or sweeter to me
Than the time I spent with you

If you fell asleep in my arms tonight
I would keep you safe and hold you so tight
Forever and all night thru

A southern girl- a miracle- an Alabama original
A southern bell- my seashell- an Alabama original

I spent the night in Birmingham
And I never got to hold your hand
But I felt something more than true

I want to make sure to thank your friend
For helping you and me understand
To meet me at the Tin Roof

A southern girl- a miracle- an Alabama original
A southern bell- my seashell- an Alabama original

She's like whiskey in a tea cup
Not afraid to stand and speak up
She's as beautiful as they come

She has a golden heart
And works hard to make it spark
With a giggle that makes me numb

A southern girl- a miracle- an Alabama original
A southern bell- my seashell- an Alabama original

Angel

I saw her walking her dog
I circled back and started to jog
I bumped her cart in aisle 9
I acted like I was buying some wine

I found me an angel to love
She flew down from heaven above
Bright stars and blue skies
Living proof of paradise

I saw my angel today
I saw my angel hooray

I saw her with another man
But she turned around and gave me a grin
One day she was teaching my kid
Next day we were laying in bed

I found me an angel to love
She flew down from heaven above
Bright stars and blue skies
Living proof of paradise

I saw my angel today
I saw my angel hooray

She said I took her friend's bar seat
I apologized and bought her a drink
We made eye contact at the local gym
We both know that's a mortal sin

I found me an angel to love
She flew down from heaven above
Bright stars and blue skies
Living proof of paradise

I saw my angel today
I saw my angel hooray

Another Day

In the beginning, there was light then mass then space and time
Time is always too short for those who need it but those who
believe will be acquitted

If the heart is strong and the mind be pure the blood will flow
and help the body cure
A soul reborn will lead the way- Another place another day

But if no hell is real then no god exist to save the ghost and the
holy spirit
The fairy tale of stories fade- Another place another day

In between, there were promises then Mary then Eve and
goddesses
He said let the tide bring them revelations for no sails travel
without winds of change

If the heart is strong and the mind be pure the blood will flow
and help the body cure
A soul reborn will lead the way- Another place another day

But if no hell is real then no god exist to save the ghost and the
holy spirit
The fairy tale of stories fade- Another place another day

In the end, there was darkness then silence then death and emptiness
Sometimes the world no longer needs a hero but those who do sing hallelujah

Artie

When Artie went away, when Artie went away
And I come down from this rage loneliness will set into my veins
I think it's getting better but how can I see clearer
When you know tricks that put me in suspense
You can take me to the edge you can sell my place to live
But I know in my heart you won't forgive
I don't know where I'm going and there's no way to explain it
I just left your peaceful world again
My bad side's growing larger it's growing like a cancer
And there's not enough of me to keep it in

When Jesus went away, when Jesus went away
He blew her into the wind leaving me behind to settle my
frustrations with my mind
Many words can't describe the empty feelings many words
can't describe the empty rooms that remind
I tried to go to sleep but I can't dream my way out now
Maybe I can somehow find a path
I tried to take a detour, but this road is getting shorter
When I let my feelings get out of hand

When Laurie went away, when Laurie went away
Everything I ever loved had let me down
I know it's for the better but how can I get stronger
When there's no one there to bring me round

Better

She will never understand I need my rest again
I try to make it clear to her that we can still be friends
I look up and see the spot that she said looks like heaven
I never second guessed her I just found something better

Better- better I found something that's better
Better- better I found someone that's better

I have an open-door policy you can come and go as you please
She lost the key I made for her, so she won't wake up my neighbors
She gave it her best shot she had a chance to be on top
Now it doesn't matter because I found something better

Better- better I found something that's better
Better- better I found someone that's better

I found someone that I can trust I found someone that I can love
She lit up my candlelight she may be my next wife
She is my candle in the wind she loves to see the devil grin
She is my brand-new lover I found something better

Better- better I found something that's better
Better- better I found someone that's better

Busy Bee

I just sent her home with her panties in her purse
Bra in her hand she was looking so perverse
Asking me when she can see me again
So, she can tell all of her family and friends
Honey, I don't want to date-ya
But honey, I'll text you late-a

Easy as ABC- Easy as 123
Ride with me babe- I'm your VIP
Easy as ABC- Easy as 123
Keep up with me babe- I'm a busy bee

Woke up this morning with my clothes on the floor
Smelling like the bar from the night before
Stumble down the hall to the bathroom door
Crawl back in bed and get you some more
Honey, I don't want to date-ya
But honey, I'll text you late-a

Easy as ABC- Easy as 123
Ride with me babe- I'm your VIP
Easy as ABC- Easy as 123
Keep up with me babe- I'm a busy bee

Can't Always Get What I Want

She sang one night in the parking lot
She dropped her notes for me on the spot
She drank one night on my balcony
She passed right out on shot number three
She drove one night just to get back home
She wrecked my car on a winding road

I can't always get what I want sometimes
But I get what I get, and I take what is mine
I can't always get what I want sometimes
But I take what I take, and I keep what I find

Her dad and her brother want to hunt me down
But they can't find me cuz I'm still out of town
I burned her clothes in a dumpster bomb
She tracked me down and then she called my mom

I can't always get what I want sometimes
But I get what I get, and I take what is mine
I can't always get what I want sometimes
But I take what I take, and I keep what I find

Can't Take It With You

We all want a peaceful life
We all seek something right
Promise me this and promise me that
Don't push me down and don't hold me back
Naked and lost as you try to survive
Living alone beats being buried alive
Can't pay my bills or cash in my checks
Can't catch my breath with your foot on my chest

Find a good place to lie when you're ready to die
Can't take it with you when it's time for goodbye

Chasing your dreams with a life contract
Works for so many if you stay on track
Forgive me for this and forgive me for that
I'm tired of hearing am I too skinny or fat

Find a good place to lie when you're ready to die
Can't take it with you when it's time for goodbye

We all want lots of silver and gold
The more we make the more we grow old

Riddle me this and riddle me that
The dog chased the cat, and the cat ate the rat

Find a good place to lie when you're ready to die
Can't take it with you when it's time for goodbye

Christmas Time (Ride On)

Christmas time is here again
It's Christmas eve at the bar this year
Christmas time is here again
It's Christmas eve and time for cheer

Ride on, Ride on
Try to find your way back home
Ride on, Ride on
Have a drink with me my dear

I remember riding on those winter roads between grandma's
house and our family home
Christmas dinner with all the kids, me and my sisters opening gifts
All the memories are still the same just a little more faded and
a little less fame
I'd like to go back and see them again one more time just tell
me when

Tis the season for memories
Tis the season for family
Silent nights by the fireplace
Drinking wine with your soulmate

Ride on, Ride on
Try to find your way back home

Ride on, Ride on
Have a drink with me my dear

I remember riding on those winter roads between grandma's
house and our family home
Christmas dinner with all the kids, me and my sisters opening gifts
All the memories are still the same just a little more faded and
a little less fame
I'd like to go back and see them again one more time just tell
me when

Ride on, Ride on
Merry Christmas to everyone
Ride on, Ride on
It Christmas time back home

Come Back Home

Can't let you leave without saying goodbye
Too many tears have poured out of my eyes
Can't let you go without ending the fight

But you know you can always come back home
And I pray that you know you're not alone

The pressures in life can produce a diamond
So, hold on tight it's your turn to shine on
A brilliant soul born one of a kind

But you know you can always come back home
And I pray that you know you're not alone

Your dreams in life will make you go
A yellow brick path made of solid gold
May you never reach the end of the road

But you know you can always come back home
And I pray that you know you're not alone

Cruel World

Our world is full of peace,
beauty, and delight
But we all seen the oddities that
creep in this peculiar paradise

Midnight Sun, Eternal Flames,
and Sleeping Pele
Blood Falls, Magnetic Hill, and
Death Valley

The wind will blow the sky will bleed
The land will shake beyond capacity
Lightning strikes a tumbleweed
Have been known to cause a great
stampede

The sun comes up and burns your skin
It's a cruel- cruel world that we live in
The universe is wearing thin
It's a cruel- cruel world that we live in

This life is full of faith, hope, and love
But we've all been bitten and puzzled to the point we can't get
enough

Bat Blizzards, Dragonflies, and Bearded Clams
Old Faithful, Asteroids, and the Dogman

The wind will blow the sky will bleed
The land will shake beyond capacity
Lightning strikes a tumbleweed
Have been known to cause a great stampede

The sun comes up and burns your skin
It's a cruel- cruel world that we live in
The universe is wearing thin
It's a cruel- cruel world that we live in

Cute As A Bug

You been around this place for a million years
But when the lights turn on you disappear
You never really been a picky eater
But you take the cake from the pic-nic table
You're more than 4,000 species strong and growing
Buzzing, flying and creepy crawling

Caught up in a spider web or under the rug
You're in so much trouble but you're cute as a bug
Hiding in the bushes or in the shrubs
You're such an agitation but you're cute as a bug

You live your life like you own the earth
Digging your home deep down in the dirt
Feeling friendly but you're making enemies
Just like a woman that you can never please
Surviving in the cracks and tiny crevices
Making haste and creating menaces

Caught up in a spider web or under the rug
You're in so much trouble but you're cute as a bug
Hiding in the bushes or in the shrubs
You're such an agitation but you're cute as a bug

Do We Date The Same Guy

Hey pretty momma did you see my face
I swear to you I don't have a date
Check my status I'm free as a bird
Despite the rumors that you may have heard

He let me slip and slide all night
He lied and lied girl hold my wine
He left me high and dry don't swipe
Tell me- tell me do we date the same guy

If there's a rhyme, then there's a reason
He lives a double life in the Caribbean
Throw him under the bus if you must
Speak the truth about what's all the fuss

He let me slip and slide all night
He lied and lied girl hold my wine
He left me high and dry don't swipe
Tell me- tell me do we date the same guy

Gentle and sweet with a deadly grin
But no complaints about that mighty chin
I heard he stands about 10 feet tall
Has Paul Bunyan sized golf balls

Don't Blame Me

You got the same rights as me to get killed for being in the wrong place at the wrong time
But I don't have the same rights as you to claim racism or a hate crime
You say I'm privileged for being white with greed
But I bleed many different colors and many different creeds

Don't blame me I'm just the pride of a revolution
Don't blame me for causing all the confusion

Don't blame me if I don't pretend to play your game
Just keep it to yourself- I'm not the one to blame
I'm not the one to blame if you feel ashamed
Don't blame me- I'm not the one to blame

They said we couldn't change the world but look what we have done
We built the greatest nation, and everyone wants some of the fun
You act like you don't want to be here because it's just not good enough
Well step aside and make room for the others that want to come

Don't blame me I'm just the pride of a revolution
Don't blame me for causing all the confusion

Don't blame me if I don't pretend to play your game
Just keep it to yourself- I'm not the one to blame
I'm not the one to blame if you feel ashamed
Don't blame me- I'm not the one to blame

I don't play a fiddle just to hear a noise
I can preach the music when you hear my voice
I don't play with matches just to start a fire
I can light you up when I feel inspired

Don't Give A Shit

I don't drive a Cadillac, but I sure been around the block
I'm not a member of the country club but I'll still play a round
of golf
I don't own a fancy boat, but I still catch a lot of fish
I don't have a pot to piss in, but I still live like I'm rich

If I didn't have such bad luck, I'd have no luck at all
I don't blame the President cuz I know it's not his fault
I'm not too old to learn new tricks I've never been one to quit
But I don't see the point of living like I give a god dam shit

I don't care about the way things are, I don't care what others
think
I don't care about your fancy dinners or the way you spend
your week
I don't care what you think of me, I don't give a country lick
I don't care if you like my songs, I don't give a god dam shit

There aint no doctor that can help me whenever I get sick
You may not like my answers when you ask about my politics
There's no one else in my life that can change my evil ways
I'm stubborn as a donkey's ass on a hot summer day

If I didn't have such bad luck, I'd have no luck at all
I don't blame the President cuz I know it's all my fault

I'm not too old to learn new tricks I've never been one to quit
I don't see the point of living like I give a god dam shit

I don't care about the way things are, I don't care what others think
I don't care about your fancy dinners or the way you spend
your week
I don't care what you think of me, I don't give a country lick
I don't care if you like my songs, I don't give a god dam shit

I can't afford a top shelf date, but I still drink around the clock
My favorite jeans got another hole so now they match my
best socks

Double Trouble

I say hey bartender - I got no
money - My card's no good -
My wife's not either
Why do you hate - When I
can't pay - I can't make - I
can't take

I say hey dancing girl - I need
a good thrill - So turn down the lights - I got dollar bills
I see you shake - It won't break - You can bake - Like a cake

You see trouble when I drink doubles
The night gets longer and my mouth gets louder
You see trouble when I drink doubles
The girls get younger and my heart beats faster

I like to drink my vodka with a double shot of Red Bull and
whiskey
Lean myself against the bar seat get back home before the
game ends

I like to drink my vodka with a double shot of Red Bull and
whiskey
Find my friends and get my car keys drive back home before
she miss me

37

I say hey big dealer - Show me a winner - Need my cards - Ace on the river
My body aches - I can't fake - Take your rake - You dirty snake

I say hey boss man – I'm feeling sad - Can't get to work - My trucks in the sand
I won't wake - Still at the lake - Leave me alone - For goodness sake

You see trouble when I drink doubles
The night gets longer and my mouth gets louder
You see trouble when I drink doubles
The girls get younger and my heart beats faster

I like to drink my vodka with a double shot of Red Bull and whiskey
Lean myself against the bar seat get back home before the game ends

I like to drink my vodka with a double shot of Red Bull and whiskey
Find my friends and get my car keys drive back home before she miss me

Dragons and Butterflies

Life can be so simple but it breaks me sometimes
I can't remember when things looked so fine
I take her to some of her favorite spots
Just to get a smile and steal a few hugs

Where mountains touch mountains and stars never fade
Dragons fly free and Kings lead the way

Dragons and butterflies one day they will meet
And life will be magical and forever free

Fly fly-fly away with me
Dragons and butterflies await in my dreams
Fly fly-fly away with me
We can live so peacefully

The time we spend together never last long enough
That's why I keep her so close to my heart
My family and friends are welcome inside
To see what makes her so happy in life

Nature meets nature and the sun sparks intrigue
Butterflies kiss and Queens keep the peace

Dragons and butterflies one day they will meet
And life will be magical and forever free

Fly fly-fly away with me
Dragons and butterflies await in my dreams
Fly fly-fly away with me
We can live so peacefully

Dream Your Life Away

I've ruined my life – I've given up – Yet I'm still so young
I am less than nothing – Let that be known by everyone
To associate with me - would only bring you down
I am no longer the way I used to be- I am no longer the class clown
I had several paths to choose from - and I walked each and every one
But I got lost within the jungle - before the setting sun
There may be more to see - but that life won't be for me
I am ending mine unnecessary- because that is all I see

Killing myself slowly with daily shots of poison
Filling up my veins with bitterness and venom
Dream your life away- Give your life away

I induce the devils medicine – he has more will to win- I let loose my grasp of life
And give up on all my dreams
Living life alone- can be so perfectly
In the dead of night- no one hears you scream
I devote myself to misery - because that is all I see

Killing myself slowly with daily shots of poison
Filling up my veins with bitterness and venom

Dream your life away- Give your life away

Drive Away

Is that your old man's pick-up truck- Parked there in my parking spot
I thought you said he was gone for the day
I know that old red tackle box- And that black and white paint job
If he sees me what a ya think he's gonna say

He's gonna say boy do you know her age- Do you want to meet my 12 guage
You might want to turn around and drive away
He's gonna say listen up here's the deal- I'm gonna make you bleed, beg and squeal
If you don't apologize and just drive away

Just drive away- Just drive away
Turn that shit around and just drive away
Well, I aint no superstar and I can't take another scar
I think I'll just turn around and drive away

Well, it might just be too late- To bring you home in this drunk stage
Do you mind If I don't walk you to the door
Let me work on my excuse- And avoid his unnecessary abuse
I think I went and broke his golden rule

He's gonna say boy do you know her age- Do you want to meet my 12 guage

You might want to turn around and drive away
He's gonna say listen up here's the deal- I'm gonna make you
bleed, beg and squeal
If you don't apologize and just drive away

Just drive away- Just drive away
Turn that shit around and just drive away
Well, I aint no superstar and I can't take another scar
I think I'll just turn around and drive away

Face Your Demons

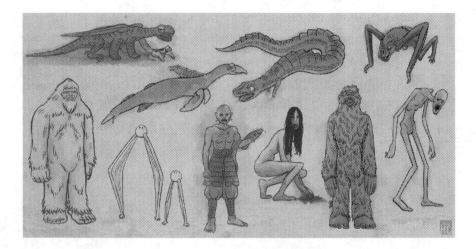

Bottoms Up, it's 12 o'clock, I'm getting ready to start
Keep pouring, keep chasing, my whisky heart

Don't unpack, I'll be right back, when the sun goes down
Here's to ya, Okele Maluna, time to drink and drown

I'm on the tv with words below me says I'm feeling deranged
I'm on the big screen you hear a loud scream I'm a pain in
the brain
You got your reasons to face your demons get yourself in line
It may not be fun to face your demons, but it will help your mind

Jim Beam whisky, can't you see me, standing on my own
You handsome devil, so sentimental, drinking all alone

I'll take another, white label Dewars, I just hit my stride
Hey bartender, call my lawyer, I'm getting ready to drive

I'm on the tv with words below me says I'm feeling deranged
I'm on the big screen you hear a loud scream I'm a pain in the
brain
You got your reasons to face your demons get yourself in line
It may not be fun to face your demons, but it will help your mind

Feel Free

She spends money like it's going out of style
You take a break to recoup your miles
Can't you see what she's trying to do
Take back what belongs to you

There's never been a better time
To stake my claim and make it mine
Can't you feel what I'm trying to say
Take an inch and be on your way

Things won't always go your way
But that is life it will be ok
Never mind what it looks like
It will heal and be just fine

Everybody wants to be someone, but nobody wants to be
no one
This world is going down in flames everyone is playing games
Feel free to walk away from me- Feel free to take your things
and leave

Feel free to walk away- Feel free to pack your things
Feel free to take your bags and leave

On a train- you will see life- aint always grand
Take it from me- the grass aint always green
On the path that-it will lead- to a better place
Plant the seeds- water your dreams- and get down on your knees
And pray to God- that he will set you free- from your chains

Feeling Free (sweet child)

Let me tell you a story about the time I ran away
I packed my bags and belongings and went off on my way
I took a greyhound bus out of Clarksburg at 7am
12 hour later I'm in South Birmingham

I met my first black man who showed me some blues
He played me his dobro and drank all my booze

The streets were dark and scary with no one around
The wind just kept on howling with desperate sounds

Oh lord, my sweet child, come home to me
I'm lost on the freeway but I'm feeling free
Oh lord, my sweet child, come home to me
Life here's not easy but I'm feeling free

I had a run-in with a lawman who made me leave town
He said this place outgrew me, so I headed south bound
My intent was meant to get there but I never arrived
I searched the world over and kept staying alive

I found my first roadblock when I turned 19
She gave me a reason to change my routine

Small bits of stardust blown down from the sky
Sing me a reason and a sweet lullaby

Oh lord, my sweet child, come home to me
I'm lost on the freeway but I'm feeling free
Oh lord, my sweet child, come home to me
Life here's not easy but I'm feeling free

Follow Him/Let It Be

You can take a seat in a stand up position
You can view the show from the front of the row
You can join your friends in the congregation
You can dream out loud when you hear the sound

Raise your hands- shout with me
Lift me up to his glory
Stomp your feet- pray with me
Follow him and let it be

You can witness Christ in his resurrection
You can praise the truth when you feel the groove
You can bear the treasures from his affliction
You can do a dance when you get a chance

Raise your hands- shout with me
Lift me up to his glory
Stomp your feet- pray with me
Follow him and let it be

Free Me

I tried to see well I guess that I
am blind
It's fine with me cuz I'm going to
keep on trying
Cuz I may disappoint my very
best friend

I want to see who you're gonna be and when
I only want you to be yourself and see
It does no good to pretend that you are free

Free lord free- lord- free lord free
Free lord free- lord - I'm free lord free
Lord, can't you see that I'm free
Free me lord- free me lord- oh lord- won't you free me

If I cannot see you my only friend
I loved you son, but it drags me down
I never felt like I feel when I'm crying
I don't care where I'm living or I'm dying

I want to see who you're gonna be and when
I only want you to be yourself and see
It does no good to pretend that you are free

Free lord free- lord- free lord free
Free lord free- lord - I'm free lord free
Lord, can't you see that I'm free
Free me lord- free me lord- oh lord- won't you free me

God Help Me

I hate to say I'm lonely
I hate to say I'm sorry
I hate to go to bed all alone

I pray for you baby
I pray for you honey
I pray that we both make it home

God help me sail away- God tell me what to say

Time helps me
Time heals me
Time can be my best friend

I love to say I love you
I love to say I hate you
I love how we spend our weekends

I try to find true love and I try just to get by, and I try, and I try
and I try
I cry for you baby and ill cry for you maybe and I cry, and I cry
and I cry

I know that you see me
I know that you hear me
I know that you won't disappear

You told me you love me
You told me you hate me
You told me that loud and clear

God help me understand- God help me be a man

I love when you smile
I love your hair style
I love when we are as one

I act like I am crazy
I act like I am insane
I act like we are in love

I try to find true love and I try just to get by, and I try, and I try
and I try
I cry for you baby and ill cry for you maybe and I cry, and I cry
and I cry

Going Down

Above the law, a judge's call, just another righteous gripe
Below the belt, nothing helps, don't believe all the hype
Playing chess, is nothing less, than a predetermined risk
A hidden hand, is nothing more, than a cold civil war
If you see my gun, you better run, I will not say twice
Listen dear let's be clear we have God given rights
Incoming…down, down, down, we are going down
Down, down, down, we hit the ground

March on order, across the border, and take a human life
They fight like hell, to read your mail, it was the perfect crime
My body my choice, raise your voice, and follow the golden rule
You must embrace, accept the grace, the rising cost of fuel
Pick your side, roll your dice, the devil will take all odds
Play your hand, fuck the white man, into the firing squad
Look out…down, down, down, we are going down
Down, down, down, we hit the ground

Good Outlaws

I never spent a night in jail, but I've been chased by the cops
I may have even broken the law, but I never did get caught
We stole clothes from JC Penny and CDs from the mall
We grew up in a nice hometown, but we acted like outlaws

We acted like we would never die and always be young
We took the good we took the bad and we turned it into fun
We saw black and we saw white we saw flashing lights
Somehow, we survived it all- We were just good outlaws

We're just good outlaws- We never meant no harm
We sometimes got out of control but we we're just good outlaws
We're just good outlaws- We keep moving along
The show goes on and we ride on- We're just good outlaws

We went to a Christmas dance, and I got into a fight
He may have only been half my size, but I made him pay the price
We took out buddy's brand-new car and used it to dine and dash
We figured out a way for free to fill up our tanks with gas

We acted like we would never die and always be young
We took the good we took the bad and we turned it into fun
We saw black and we saw white we saw flashing lights
Somehow, we survived it all- We were just good outlaws

We're just good outlaws- We never meant no harm
We sometimes got out of control but we we're just good outlaws
We're just good outlaws- We keep moving along
The show goes on and we ride on- We're just good outlaws

Goodbye To Romance

Mistakes I made a few - It began when I met you
Don't argue with a fool- It only proves there are two

Hinderance- Deliverance
Good Riddance- Indifference

I will wonder why until the day I die
I will always be until it's time to leave
Goodbye my darling- Goodbye to thee
Goodbye my romance- Goodbye my grief

Trust it never fails- Truth and honor prevails
Unique It's not ideal- (When it's) just like everyone else
Ask me no questions- I'll tell you no lies
Bring me my dinner- Just like my last wife

Hinderance- Deliverance
Good Riddance- Indifference

I will wonder why until the day I die
I will always be until it's time to leave
Goodbye my darling- Goodbye to thee
Goodbye my romance- Goodbye my grief

Heavens Trail

I ride the midnight train, I have a million miles to go- I know
I hear the crazy train, I hear it calling out my name- I'm insane
I see the tracks ahead, I get on board to follow them- to the end

I have a one-way ticket on the iron horse
I'm hell on wheels but I'm not off course
I'm hell on wheels but I'm not derailed

Faster than a speeding bullet
More powerful than a locomotive
I'm hell on wheels but I'm not derailed

When the stars line up and the stairs prevail
There is a place for you and me on heavens trail

I ride on hells highway, I don't have far to go- I know
I hear the angels voice, I hear the songs of rejoice- and joy
I see the cloudy skies, they bring tears to my eyes- goodbye

I have to climb the stairs to heaven
I don't have wings but I'm on a mission
I don't have wings, but I play to win

The moon will guide you thru the darkness
The sun will shine for you with the brightness
I don't have wings, but I play to win

When the stars line up and the stairs prevail
There is a place for you and me on heavens trail

Ho Ho Ho

He's rocking his new 4-wheel drive on the ice-covered roads
Family and friends and little ones dashing thru the snow
He gets so sad and lonely when the season comes to end
He gets so sad and lonely when the children don't pretend

Ho ho ho on the radio- he loves his Christmas songs
Ho ho ho on the radio- bringing presents all night long

He's bringing cheer to the whole wide world on his red rocket ship
Dasher, Dancer, and Prancer, Cupid and all the rest
He gets so sad and lonely when the snow begins to melt
He gets so sad and lonely when he can't find his elf

Ho ho ho on the radio- he loves his Christmas songs
Ho ho ho on the radio- bringing presents all night long

Candy canes and mistle toes, cookies and chocolate milk
Bing Crosby and Mariah Carey singing the first Noel
He gets so sad and lonely when the jingle bells don't ring
He gets so sad and lonely when the angels above don't sing

Ho ho ho on the radio- he loves his Christmas songs
Ho ho ho on the radio- bringing presents all night long

Ho ho ho on the radio- singing that Christmas cheer
Ho ho ho on the radio- counting 7-8-9 reindeer

I Must Pray

I hear the music in my head- a
pounding in my heart
The vision of a painting- my
memories sold as art
I feel the soul of a dragon-
breathing fire in my words
The wisdom of a scholar- that
teaches nouns and verbs

Oh lord I must pray- to make it
thru the day
I pray for some hope and
some faith
Oh lord I must pray- to keep the wrongs away
I pray that you keep me strong and safe

I wrote my heart inside out- cried myself to sleep
The rain sent me a message- to turn the other cheek
Touch your hair with my fingers- rest my arm on your body
The bridge is a connection- between the sound you embody

Oh lord I must pray- to make it thru the day
I pray for some hope and some faith
Oh lord I must pray- to keep the wrongs away
I pray that you keep me strong and safe

If It's So Easy

She is smart and she is pretty – uh huh
She likes me and thinks I am witty – uh huh
As soon as I get one then I want the other
I take one or two and then another

If it's so easy, why do I feel so lonely – tonight
God dam I still love her plenty- alright
I don't know why it hurt me so much
But fuck her and the whole god dam bunch

She's a diamond in the bar – uh huh
The sky's the limit and I am the star- uh huh
We connect before we drift- too far
We combine and then we split- apart

If it's so easy why do I feel so lonely – tonight
God dam I still love her plenty- alright
I don't know why it hurt me so much
But fuck her and the whole god dam bunch

Dads look at me like they want to fight me- uh huh
When she walks by it drives them all crazy- uh huh
Moms troll her like she is a donut
They get jealous and then you know what

If My Dog Could Talk

If my dog could talk
He would tell a story that
would make you blush
He would say some words
and some cool stuff
That he has seen in his life

If my dog could talk
He would write a book and
go on tour
He would tell you about the
people that he adores
And that he got to bite

If my dog could talk
He would say some things that you would not believe
He would tell you about the cards up his master's sleeve
And the games he plays at night

If my dog could talk
He would open his mouth and play a flute
He would present his case and tell the truth
And describe a life of crime

I know what you're thinking, you think I'm real sick
But I know what he saw made him grow up real quick
You ask how do I know, well let me tell you son
It only took 3 years for my dog to turn 21

Inside The Mind Of A Madman

I can't see straight, and I don't know where I am
The sky is dark, and I hear the sounds of the dammed
The cries are loud, but the silence is louder
The lightening rides the storm and cuts the power

Such a view from inside the zoo- Feed the animals by hand
It's getting late inside the gates- Inside the mind of a madman

The guards fall asleep, and the inmates open the gates
But the tortured souls that remain cannot escape
One by one piece by piece my thoughts begin to twist
My future plans and my memories cannot co-exist

Such a view from inside the zoo- Feed the animals by hand
It's getting late inside the gates- Inside the mind of a madman

Johnny Boy

Thru peace and love we made the world
Thru hate and war we fought like hell
Hell- hell we fought like hell
Times like this we bid farewell
On the front lines we made our will
Oh, Johnny boy oh Johnny boy please come home
Oh, Johnny boy oh Johnny boy come back home

Brother my brother you fought so well
Obey your master it's time to kill
Kill-kill it's time to kill
There is smoke on the water there is blood on the field
Your time away from us became fulfilled
Oh, Johnny boy oh Johnny boy please come home
Oh, Johnny boy oh Johnny boy come back home

The pledge of allegiance the home of the brave
You gained your freedom and stripes today
Day-Day gained your stripes today
Oh, Johnny boy oh Johnny boy please come home
Oh, Johnny boy oh Johnny boy come back home

Johnny Cash

I wish I was more like Johnny but I'm not- I stay up late, gamble, and I drink a lot
I dress all in black and play my Martin guitar- I can't stand the daylight and I'm afraid of the dark
I become weak when I'm sad but I'm strong as an ox- Mean as a grizzly and slick as a fox
I don't make my bed but I have lot to cover- My songs keep me warm just like a ring of fire
I like heavy metal music and the sound of gospel- Drums of thunder and words from the bible
I'm just like my daddy but he's more polite- Trust me boy when I say I know how to fight
I had blood on my hands since I was 18- Gods gonna cut me down if you know what I mean

I'm tall, dark and handsome just like Johnny Cash- If you don't like my songs you can kiss my white ass
I'm rough, tough and lonesome just like Johnny was- If you don't like my ways you can die just because
I wish I was more like Johnny Cash but I'm not- To tell you the truth aint nobody in this whole wide world that can sing the working man blues- Just like Johnny Cash

I've been everywhere man that I want to be- Travelling the world alone on a killing spree

I share with my friends but I know what is mine- I live on the razors edge when I walk the line

I float like a butterfly and sting like a bee- You may be quick but you can't beat me

I wrote more than 1,000 songs lines- About drinking, smoking and coping with life

But the all-mighty good lord up above - Gave me a voice that only a mother could love

I'm like the devil when the weather gets hot- I'll sing like a canary if I ever get caught

I got a mouth from the gutter to smoke with my pot- I'm kind of like Johnny Cash but I'm sure the hell not

I'm tall, dark and handsome just like Johnny Cash- If you don't like my songs you can kiss my white ass

I'm rough, tough and lonesome just like Johnny was- If you don't like my ways you can die just because

I wish I was more like Johnny Cash but I'm not- To tell you the truth aint nobody in this whole wide world that can sign the working man blues- Just like Johnny Cash

Just Close Your Eyes

Now that the road I'm on is winding down
An apparition festival through hell I shall ride
With your life on the line and your fingers slipping fast
Breaking off of company so no relationship can last

Because it aint no fun to lose when you're having so much fun
It aint no fun to lose it in the barrel of a gun
While you're kicking up a storm don't forget about my life
No one can live forever I seen that many times

You're falling off the world too bad you can't fly
Life is full of stress no desire to progress

You see your life pass you by before you in a glimpse of an eye
You see your life going by too fast to deny
You feel your life giving in and it aint supposed to end
Just close your eyes and forget about your sins

Blackness brings no colors into the skies
A disillusioned voyage into uncharted grounds
When your heart no longer pumps but you try to make a living
Losing all your memories and you hope that gods forgiving

Because it aint no fun to fight it when your living life so well
It aint no fun to fight it if you lose you go to hell

While you're running for your life don't forget to stop and pray
Evil changes peoples minds like night turns into day
You're falling off the world too bad you can't fly
Life is full of stress no desire to progress

You see your life pass you by before you in a glimpse of an eye
You see your life going by too fast to deny
You feel your life giving in and it aint supposed to end
Just close your eyes and forget about your sins

Living In A Dream

I see her- I want her- but how do I know if I like her
I like her- I kiss her- but how do I know if I love her

The answer is in my heart
She's my shining star

Am I right- Am I wrong
Seems I'm living in the seams
Am I awake- Am I asleep
Seems I'm living in a dream

I love her- I adore her- but how do I know if I marry her
I marry her- I live with her- but how do I keep up with her

The answer has been unlocked
The life that I embark

Am I right- Am I wrong
Seems I'm living in the seams
Am I awake- Am I asleep
Seems I'm living in a dream

I'm happy- I'm delighted- the future is looking bright
She smiles- she giggles- I want that the rest of my life

The answer has been solved
My love goes on beyond

Living Like A Country Song

Woke up early just to feed my dog- Drink some water and go for a jog
Rub my eyes and clear my head- Start my day the way the doctor said
Take my treatments to help me withdraw- Hard times boy I seen it all
Woke up wrong on the side of the tracks- I was hungry and looking for scraps
Living large with an appetite- For fast women and crazy nights
Down the hatch lock up the boos- Tough times boy shred them blues

I never thought I would live so long- I never thought I could be so strong
After all that I did wrong- I'm still living like a country song

Still living like a country song- Out all night til the crows come home
Living life like a country song- Raising Cain from dusk til dawn

Still living like a country song- It's blowing up just like a bomb
Living like a country song- Country roads is where I belong

My truck has an American flag- The bumper says I love the Jags

Trained my dog to ride shotgun- I eat my steaks and burgers well done
I found religion in my back seat- True love never taste so sweet
My papa worked for the state police- His buddies chased me up and down the street
Hard times are tough to beat- I was hell bound and felt the heat
So I turned over a brand new leaf- Now look at me I'm back on my feet

I never thought I would live so long- I never thought I could be so strong
After all that I did wrong- I'm still living like a country song

Still living like a country song- Out all night til the crows come home
Living life like a country song- Raising Cain from dusk til dawn

Still living like a country song- It's blowing up just like a bomb
Living like a country song- Country roads is where I belong

Mean Streak

Fires and diamonds and killers and lust
Won't break me down like it did in the past
Trying to come out from where I was last
Giants and lions and man eating cats
Can't take away your lies are in fact
Don't you look at me now

Stay away from my mean streak
A terrible frightening place to be
Sometimes it brews inside of me
So stay away from my mean streak

The sins and scars of tragedy
Flourish in the eyes for all to see
Voices of my past ghost will speak
The truth and honor of it all
As I brace for the fall
And I'll never see you again

I'll never come home again
Please don't follow me home
So stay away from my mean streak
A horrible raging place to be
The turmoil breathes inside of me
So stay away from my mean streak

Had such high hopes of destiny
Stripped away for all to see
The reminders of all the memories
The good and evil of it all
As I brace for the fall

You'll never see me again
I'll never come home again
Please don't follow me home

Mama

You held my hand when I came into this world
Taught me to fly just like a mama bird
Walked with me and took me to a bridge
Gave me wings to jump off from the edge

You help with my mind when I can't think
You bring me wine when I need a drink

Mama- ooooooh Mama you're always there for me

When I fell down you picked me up once again
Taught tough love so I could learn my lesson
If I cried, you made sure I wasn't alone
Knowing where I'm from is all I ever known

You are my eyes when I can't see
You bring me sunshine when I'm in need

Mama- ooooooh Mama you're always there for me

Moonshine

We have a game day tradition
down a long country road
On a cold Winters Day, it goes
down like a flame
We have a proud state of mind
and a coal miner's soul
We got whiskey and beer now
let's go Mountaineers!

You got to find your young-ins, pack up their dam stuff
Head on out of town in your old beat up truck
You got to drive thru the night to get past all the cops
Stop for some coffee at the new Bucky's spot

You got to make your pay by the hillbilly way
In the starlight and the moonshine
You got to make your dime in the nick of time
In the parking lot with some moonshine

We have a game day tradition down a long country road
On a cold Winters Day, it goes down like a flame
We have a proud state of mind and a coal miner's soul
We got whiskey and beer now let's go Mountaineers!

You got your family and friends, they all depend on you
You mash the sugar and grain for 140 proof
You have a home in the hills a secret recipe
Cooks pure as the snow with a taste you can't beat

You got to make your pay by the hillbilly way
In the starlight and the moonshine
You got to make your dime in the nick of time
In the parking lot with some moonshine

Mountain Mama

I try to find my way home
Where I belong
I try to find my way thru
The winding road

Closer to nature
Cascade waters
Cool mountain streams

Closer to heaven
Mountain legend
Leads you far away

Seneca Rocks- Dolly Sods- West by God
She's my mountain mom

Mama- Mama
I'm coming home

Closer to nature
Hard working neighbors
A great place to escape

Closer to heaven
Starlight impressions
Tree shadowed landscapes

Coopers Rock- Spruce Knob- West by God
She's my mountain mom

Mama- Mama
I'm coming home

Murder

Dressing is a bad obsession that cuts off circulation
Stab your victim with a fork like a giant steps on a boy

Oh, the pain, the pain of rotting within
Slowly distorting the facts, you once believed in

Help, murder I cry, bit no one comes to save
Oh lord, how long must I call, I shout to you in vain
Drowning us in sorrow, taking our breath away
Like eagles they come swooping down and pounce upon their
prey

Licking little salt mines from a silver spoon pepper lice have
poisoned natures perfect food
Ghost clouds drop their hot spicy rain as the minerals in the
earth choke you with pain

Oh, the pain, the pain of rotting within
Slowly distorting the facts, you once believed in

Help, murder I cry, but no one comes to save
Oh lord, how long must I call, I shout to you in vain
Drowning in the sorrow, taking our breath away
Like eagles they come swooping down and pounce upon
their prey

My Buddy Zakk

I was born in a coal mine- I grew up strong
I moved to the city- That's when it all went wrong- when it all
went wrong
I met Uncle Johnny- He painted the walls
He told me his vision- It wasn't worth a dime at all- not a dime
at all

That's when I counted on my fingers- and I did the math
My life just wasn't adding up- so I rolled the dice again- baby
That's when I met my buddy Zakk

Oh, me and Zakk and the Alley Cats we went on to be
The best 5-piece hippy freak band that you have ever seen
We played the blues- we never lose
We played all night- we played for you

Oh, we rode the tracks never looked back going city to city
Singing songs playing along finding our destiny
We played the blues- we never lose
We played all night- we played for you

The first time I met her- She wore her pants so tight
I could see her religion- Oh my what a sight- oh what a sight

We made good friends- We made good lovers
But in the end- I could never really trust her- never really trust her

That's when I counted my blessings- and I tried to subtract
But all those lies kept adding up- so I rolled the dice again- baby
That's when I met my buddy Zakk

Oh, me and Zakk and the Alley Cats we went on to be
The best 5-piece hippy freak band that you have ever seen
We played the blues- we never lose
We played all night- we played for you

Oh, we rode the tracks never looked back going city to city
Singing songs playing along finding our destiny
We played the blues- we never lose
We played all night- we played for you

My Checks All Go Bad

Sitting down at the kitchen table, I got the news today
My banker called said I got no money, and my house is underpaid
I called my momma to ask for help, but the river has all gone dry
I think I used up all nine lives, as I wait here to die

Working hard for little pay
Spending more than I can make
I got that monkey on my back

When it rains and it pours
And the skies begin to storm
That's when my checks all go bad

I take a penny from the cookie jar, I got no more dough
I can't look my family in the eyes, I got nothing left to show
I took my chance at monopoly, but I never got pass Go
My utilities got shut off, and my pipes no longer flow

Bringing home less each day
Spending more than I get paid
And all my wells run out of gas

When it rains cats and dogs
And I get fired from my job
That's when my checks all go bad

Driving down highway 10, on my way to Ala-bam
To see this girl I met last week, in South Birmingham
I drove my new pick-up truck, running low on fumes
Can't wait to see my baby, and smell that sweet perfume

My Little Reflection

I see the sunlight in her eyes
It brings vision into my life
May her flowers never spoil
And her heart never cry

I feel proud to hold her hand
And write her name in the sand
May she smile in her sleep
And her dreams be in command

All I see is her reflection- rising from the light
May her future be like the sun- shining bright in the sky

I hear the wind blowing thru
It brings rain in the afternoon
May the sun and moon unite
And the skies return to blue

I taste the wine from the river
And eat the bread for my dinner
May the shelter provide me comfort
And the food become my hunger

All I see is her reflection- like the writing on the wall
May her future be like a tree- growing steady firm and tall

My Oh My

Well, the first thing I did when I got out of bed was to call my very best friend
Well, the first thing I did before I went to bed was to pray for another day like this

We went down to the Blackwater Falls with my dog and a cooler of beer
We sat on the hood, and we howl at the moon as we wait for the stars to appear

My oh my what a wonderful place down by the river and lake
My oh my what a beautiful day to ride in my old Chevrolet

Times like this we reminiscence about the beauty in the sky
Times like this we reminiscence about the stories of my life

The sun shines true on the western view where the birds and the eagles flew
A river runs thru, and the trees all grew oh the city folk don't have a clue

I sat on a stump with my red dixie cup and the campfire kept us safe
We hoot and we holler and strummed on the fender as the coyotes sing and play

My oh my what a wonderful place down by the river and lake
My oh my what a beautiful day to ride in my old Chevrolet

Times like this we reminiscence about the beauty in the sky
Times like this we reminiscence about the stories of my life

Never Say Goodbye

I'm going away for a very long- long time
It won't be long until the fat lady sings her song
I'm going away to the house up in the sky
It troubles me for you to worry about my life

I held your hand for a very long- long time
It won't be long until I leave you all behind
I'm filling up my grievances with the judge
It fills my heart to be empty when I'm done

Read my rights- hold me tight never say goodbye
Life is grand- like a band trying to get by
Kiss my cheek- speak your peace never say goodbye
Farewell to thee- let it be trying to get by

I lived my life for a very long- long time
It took me places up and down the line
I'm grazing land to find my place to lay
It calms my sea to swim into the waves

Read my rights- hold me tight never say goodbye
Life is grand- like a band trying to get by
Kiss my cheek- speak your peace never say goodbye
Farewell to thee- let it be trying to get by

No Devil No Evil
No Consequences

The devil gave a speech to all of his dominions
He said the time has come to empty out the prisons
He started buying judges and crooked politicians
Making silly promises causing much division

Right is wrong and wrong is right
Light for dark and dark for light
Sleight of hand and proposition
No devil, no evil, no consequence

Cold is hot and hot is cold
Low is high and high is low
Palm the cards and dirty tricks
No devil, no evil, no consequence

The villagers lived in great temptation
Chasing gossip, greed, and provocation
They lost the spotlight of their attention
And focused more on discontentment

Right is wrong and wrong is right
Light for dark and dark for light
Sleight of hand and proposition
No devil no evil no consequence

Cold is hot and hot is cold
Low is high and high is low
Palm the cards and dirty tricks
No devil, no evil, no consequence

The devil sleeps inside of you, for he knows the evil that you do
He pulls the covers over and whispers all night thru
He hungers for your weakness, and the taste of your stew
You have to wake up in the garden and denounce his pursuit
He teaches dissension, dispute, and factions, enmities, carousing, impurities, and thought distractions
He hides behind poetry, art, music, and human understanding using weapons of polished swords, deafen roars, daggers, knives, red suits and horns

No Place Like Home

There is no place in the world that I would rather be
Than home on the couch with my family
On a cold December night with a warm fireplace
On a hot August day with a cool summer breeze
Like the flight of an eagle and the grace of a deer
I got the wit of a fox and the strength of a bear

There is no place like home- Only one thing that I know
I can always find the way- To my home sweet home
There is no place like home- Only one thing that I know
You can always come with me- To my home sweet home

I climb down from the mountain and set my soul free
To do the things I done and see the things I seen
There is no place like home to search for a memory
So I look to the past to find the best of me
There is no place like the road to search for harmony
So I pray to the lord to find the missing piece

There is no place like home- Only one thing that I know
I can always find the way- To my home sweet home
There is no place like home- Only one thing that I know
You can always come with me- To my home sweet home

No Way I Can Change

Take me down this road
Help me find my soul
When I last saw your face
I lost my self-control

Believe in fantasy
Magic in my dreams
Dragons are make believe
But they keep me company

There is no one I can blame
There is no way I can change
For the better

Brave birds just like these
Flying high above the trees
Can see the things to come
We want so desperately

Believe in fantasy
Magic in my dreams
Dragons are make believe
But they keep me company

There is no one I can blame
There is no way I can change
For the better

One Chance Left

Same old fight on a different night a new painting on the wall
The current swifter for another drifter who's heart won't let him fall
There's trouble in this big old town and they don't know who
to blame
No money but we still live well better than those who slave
Another paid customer turning away

On the run but we stay put never want to leave this place
I should be smarter I should know better but I do it anyway

I have one chance left to change my ways
I have one chance left to mend the pain
I have one chance left and I'm never coming back

Black and blue they are hunting you they will never get you alive
Some are drinking some are smoking it was the perfect crime
The West is best don't care what happens next

On the run but we stay put never want to leave this place
I should be smarter I should know better but I do it anyway

I have one chance left to change my ways
I have one chance left to mend the pain
I have one chance left and I'm never coming back

One Hearted Man

Hey, let's go down to New Orleans and find myself another girl
to love
I'm trying my best to understand why my life is only a dream-
only a dream

Take me down to the bright city lights where the girls all stay
out all night
Dancing queens and roof top bars music clubs and Hollywood
stars

I bought her a big ol house and I gave her an honest life
But she doesn't have a clue in what I try to do
I need my beer and I need my space I need my guns and my
get aways

I got nothing to hide I got time on my side
I like being bad but I'm a one hearted man

I bought her a big ol ring and I gave her a king size bed
But she doesn't find the humor when I try to amuse her
When I roll my dice and I play my cards
And leave my dog shit out in the yard

I got nothing to hide I got time on my side
I like being bad but I'm a one hearted man

Only The Dead Have Seen
The End Of The War

We pour out one shot for those left behind
Stand up and honor those that have died
You got food on your table and clothes on your back
The freedom to work for an honest paycheck
There's nothing more stylish than a soldier's uniform
Bloody from fighting and serving his home

You got to keep on moving there's no time to mourn
Only the dead have seen the end of the war
You got to keep on breathing and bury the sword
Only the dead have seen the end of the war

Heroes have come and heroes have gone
Better count your sweet blessings if you ever meet one
Generals give orders and advice at great cost
No winners or losers only two that have lost
Stand for the flag and take off that dam hat
Put your hands on your chest and cheer for them old Hellcats!

You got to keep on moving there's no time to mourn
Only the dead have seen the end of the war
You got to keep on breathing and bury the sword
Only the dead have seen the end of the war

Out Of Control

Let me tell you a story about the time I met Jim Beam
He shook my hand when I was only 17
I licked my lips and poured myself a glass
He held me down and began to kick my ass

I was in another place- Searching for my soul
I was in another town- Far away from home
I was looking for a friend- Searching high and low
I was down and out- I was out of control

Let me tell you a story about the time I ran away
I lost my grip and I had no where to stay
The nights were getting cold and my days were all gone
Drinking the bottle from the day I was born

I was in another place- Searching for my soul
I was in another town- Far away from home
I was looking for a friend- Searching high and low
I was down and out- I was out of control

Paid Attention

You blow the horn like I blow off steam
You keep my engine running smooth and clean
You rev me up and you rub me down
You keep your hands moving all around

I told you once, I'll tell you again
Listen up try to comprehend
You taste better than a Georgia peach
I'll drive you faster than a Hennessy

I paid attention when you cleaned up nice
It came down to the sticker price
I paid attention to your engine lights
It came down to the free test ride

You hold me tight like a drinking cup
You put me down when you had enough
You roll those eyes when you feel my touch
You kick and scream when I hit the spot

I told you once, I'll tell you again
Hear my voice try to understand
You taste better than a warm muffin
I'll drive you faster than a McLaren

I paid attention when you cleaned up nice
It came down to the sticker price
I paid attention to your engine lights
It came down to the free test ride

Pay To Play

I keep on driving I'm on a one-way street - I can't be tamed I'm on an independent streak
I'm a dragon I'm a fire breathing beast - I prey on the innocent the sick and the weak

Never surrender your dignity - It's a pay to play corrupt society

I sit on the porch and watch the evening news – It's all about your political views
It's a million hits on your twitter account - But that don't explain why your vote don't count

See something say something - But only if you can agree with me

The day will come for all humanity - When they come for us and we face the beast
When they strip you down and try to demean

Never surrender your dignity- It's a pay to play corrupt society

You sit on the couch and watch the MTV - It corrupts your mind with indecency
Now it's all about the tik- tik- tok - Whatever happened to my Christian rock

China sees get on your knees- It's a pay to play corrupt society
We support the police and our military – strong borders and economy
But now I'm worried about my 401 – everything I saved is almost gone

See something say something - But only if you can agree with me

The day will come for all humanity - When they come for us and we face the beast
When they strip you down and try to demean
Never surrender your dignity- It's a pay to play corrupt society

Power

There's a man on the run- he can't find his way home
He tries and he tries- but the light will not shine
He lost his sight in the war- but he gained so much more
From the lives that he saved- and received from his grace
He got the power from it all- as he learned his new call
He was standing tall- when the lord became his eyes and he saw

He climbed over the hills- and he heard what he heard
The laughter and the joy- he knew as a boy
His heart was getting filled- with his hope and thrills
The lord gave him the gift- to solve his conflicts
He got the power from it all- as he learned his new call
He was standing tall- when the lord became his eyes and he saw

He is trying to be- what he wanted to be
He tries to escape- the things that he seen
He is trying to get home- to his love and his soul
Use his power to heal- the things that they stole
He got the power from it all- as he learned his new call
He was standing tall- when the lord became his eyes and he saw

He got the power to preach and sing melodies
He got the power from it all – as he learned his new call
He was standing tall – when the lord became his eyes and he saw

Raising Kids

Raising kids goes slow at first but once it comes it goes by so fast
School dances and math homework I wish I knew how to make it last
My kids are growing my net worth spending time and spending cash
Down the aisle and off to work time goes by in just a flash

On the first day that I held them I knew there was something more
Tiny fingers and big brown eyes filled my heart with joy
Nothing sweeter as a child grows than when they smile at you so proud
Calls you mom or dad and holds your hand even with their friends around

There was a time I went to church back when I was living pure
Now I thank God every night since the day my kids were born
Raising kids are the living proof of God's presence in this world
The greatest gift to our lives that ever could occur

When they fall down and start to cry, we want to cry too
But we play tough to teach them stuff and help them make it thru

Well, I'm proud to be a single dad even when I am all alone
I may not be the perfect man, but I know where I come from
Well, I'm proud to be a simple man working from 9 to 5
I may not be the President, but I know how to survive

Remember The Last Time

Every night she goes out to the bars
Rolls up like some Hollywood superstar
Whiskey glasses as far as you can see
Darling them bottles aren't for free

Better slow up- slow down don't you make a scene
Remember the last time that you drank Jim Beam
Better sit up- sit down I know that routine
Remember the last time I had to intervene

She is right on time every day
That's when her night gets underway
She dances like no one is watching her
That sweet taste makes her want it more

Fool me- shame me you drink more than your share
Remember the last time you lost your underwear
Told you- showed you that I still care
Remember the last time you got so impaired

Remember Yesterday (911)

Well, I remember that day just like it was yesterday
I went to work like so many others
But not every American got to come home that day

Well, I still see images of people jumping out of buildings
When I lay down and close my eyes at night
And hear the voices of those heroes saying
Let's fight back when they took down that airline flight

Well, I remember yesterday
Memories that won't go away
I remember everything
Heroes that ran toward the flame

If we lose our way just look at the beauty and the majesty
There is freedom in this life apple pie and Jesus Christ
Always stand up for your flag never forget those who died
so sad

Well, I remember yesterday
Memories that won't go away
I remember everything
Heroes that ran toward the flame

I remember yesterday
A day that will live in infamy
I remember everything
The way the country used to be

Well, I remember that day just like it was yesterday
When America was bleeding, we all came together just like a family
The man told the world the people who knocked down these buildings
They're all going to hear from all of us soon enough when we let our freedom ring

Well, I remember yesterday
Memories that won't go away
I remember everything
Heroes that ran toward the flame

I remember yesterday
A day that will live in infamy
I remember everything
the way our country used to be

Ride Me

She's got the mind of the devil with the heart of an angel
A soul filled with speed keeps her company
She's dressed up to kill with a lesbo thrill
Her motor keeps running like a fast machine

You got to live free, die free, pop the clutch and let it be
You got to hold on, stay strong, let it hum and have some fun
You got to grab me, hold me, and ride me home tonight
Kick start me, squeeze me, and hear my engine whine

High heels and thighs on a Saturday night
The dance floor takes her away from me
Take a chance and find your true romance
Chase your miles and catch your dreams

You got to live free, die free, pop the clutch and let it be
You got to hold on, stay strong, let it hum and have some fun
You got to grab me, hold me, and ride me home tonight
Kick start me, squeeze me, and hear my engine whine

She's a runaway model that goes full throttle
A soft tail pan head from down the street
She's cool as ice and gets cleaned up nice
Shows her crack on the hard concrete

Ride The Lightning

I would move a mountain just to buy you an island
Climb the tallest tower and walk a hundred miles
I would play dumb like a clown just to see you smile
Skip a day of work just to keep you safe and sound

I'd be your wisdom, zeal, and power
Pick you a million flowers
Put them in a vase
So, you cold smell them again tomorrow

I'd ride the lightning in the sky
Catch a million fire flies
Put them in a bottle
So, it shines for you at night

I'd ride the lightning like a jet airplane
Take a bullet to the heart
I'd buy you almost anything
Just to play my part

I'd ride the lightning like a jet airplane
Fly you around the world
Buy you almost anything
And let you keep the change

I'd put all my luck on red just to give you thrills
Cancel all my calls and pay off all your bills
I would grant you any wish if I held the lamp
Give you peace and fortune and gifts to unwrap

I'd be your wisdom, zeal, and power
Pick you a million flowers
Put them in a vase
So, you could smell them again tomorrow

I'd ride the lightning in the sky
Catch a million fire flies
Put them in a bottle
So, it shines for you at night

I'd ride the lightning like a jet airplane
Take a bullet to the heart
I'd buy you almost anything
Just to play my part

I'd ride the lightning like a jet airplane
Fly you around the world
Buy you almost anything
And let you keep the change

Roll Me If You're Feeling Lucky

One step back is one step closer
Hit me first and I'll hit you harder
Don't talkback and keep it silent
Prove my guilt and then my innocent
Lie to me and I'll trust you lesser
Be good to me and I'll act much better
Rescue me and set me free
Save my life like a cat in a tree

Don't take my kindness for my weakness
Its just a flower of my goodness
Cuddle with me and be my honey
Roll me once if you're feeling lucky
Roll me roll me roll me- roll me if you're feeling lucky
Sorry- sorry- sorry, sorry that you lost me

Come to me and I'll take your further
Spend time with me and I'll make you richer
First, we drink and then we buy it
Nights with you well it hurts my wallet

Don't take my kindness for my weakness
It's just a flower of my goodness
Cuddle with me and be my honey
Roll me once if you're feeling lucky

Roll me roll me roll me- roll me if you're feeling lucky
Sorry- sorry- sorry, sorry that you lost me

The first day for the rest of my life
Brings me peace and quiet nights
Trust and honor and friendly comments
Love thy neighbor and all that comes with it

Don't take my kindness for my weakness
It's just a flower of my goodness
Cuddle with me and be my honey
Roll me once if you're feeling lucky
Roll me roll me roll me- roll me if you're feeling lucky
Sorry sorry sorry- sorry that you lost me

Save Me

Down in the valley where I lay my weary head
I look to the sky and pray
Roll me some honey and serve me some bread
Spreading the news along the way
Clouds lift me up to the promise land
Lord, won't you take my hand
Knock on the door hello my dear friend
It's time to make your amends

Oh lord I'm on fire but I don't want to be
Save me my father hold on to thee
Open the door can't you take just one more
Untangle me you can trust me my lord
Save me my father hold on to thee
Trust me my brother you answered my plea

An image from heaven on the arm of your sleeve
Raise your voice shout from your knees
Wine with your dinner makes you drunk all the time
Amen my darling I'm feeling just fine

Oh lord I'm on fire but I don't want to be
Save me my father hold on to thee
Open the door can't you take just one more
Untangle me you can trust me my lord
Save me my father hold on to thee
Trust me my brother you answered my plea

Shots

I'm looking for a place for
me to hang around
There aint too many places
to go in this here town
They made the last call for
alcohol
And all hell broke loose as
I recall

Shots went up and shots went down
Some hit the wall, and some hit the ground
It's time to grab me one and have some fun

Shot- shot- I took a shot across the bow
It knocked me down, but I got back up somehow
Shot- shot- I took a shot of Crown
It knocked me down, but I got back up somehow

I got chased by the cops in my mini van
I ran out of gas, so I jumped out and ran
I hid in a dumpster for 13 hours straight
When the dogs sniffed me out, I was feeling disgraced

Shots went up and shots went down
Some hit the wall, and some hit the ground
It's time to grab me one and have some fun

Shot- shot- I took a shot across the bow
It knocked me down, but I got back up somehow
Sho- shot- I took a shot of Crown
It knocked me down, but I got back up somehow

Some Old Day

Some old day when my girl is grown
I'll be old and all alone
But that's ok cuz I had my yesterday
Yesterday will never fade
I replenish it with lemonade
Swimming in the pool on a hot summer day
Some old day when she moves away
Some old day when I'm old and grey
She will say hey dad I still love you
She may marry but in the end
I'll always be her biggest fan
I will set her free and let her be
Some old day when she leaves me
I'll look back at history
But that's ok cuz I had my yesterday
When we were young, and life was full
Spent the days skipping school
Eating cold ice cream along the way
I spent my days watching her
Swim and dance play and laugh
It's all part of life and its ok
My little girl is getting wise
All grown up before my eyes

Prettiest little thing you could ever see
Some old day when my girl is grown
I'll be old and all alone
But its ok cuz I had my yesterday

Something Just For You

I heard lots of stories about you coming home
But when I heard your voice, I knew you were the one
I first saw your face when you walked into the room
My heart skipped a beat and the time it just flew

I tried for so long to find the one for me
But all of this time you stood where I could see

Write me a song and make it just for me
Something sweet and something true just like its meant to be
Sing me a song that I can hum along to
Something soft and something dear something just for you

Too many times I just drove all night long
Alone, tired, and confused it all just seemed so wrong
But you answered my prayers and brought me something more
You took my insecurity and set my heart assure

I tried for so long to find the golden words
But all of this time you just spoke what we heard

Write me a song and make it just for me
Something sweet and something true just like its meant to be
Sing me a song that I can hum along to
Something soft and something dear something just for you

Sometimes You Just Should

Did you ever wonder just how things would go
If you did not see the sun rise in time to see it glow
Sometimes life's too much sometimes not enough
Sometimes less is good sometimes you just should

Sometimes you just should, I'd like to think I would
Sometimes you just should stop to see the good- oh man

When I can't find the time to say how are you
I've been working way too much so I grab one and drink two
Sometimes I drink too much sometimes not enough
Sometimes more is good sometimes you just should

Sometimes you just should, I'd like to think I would
Sometimes you just should, stop to see the good, oh-man

Sometimes I talk too much sometimes not enough
Hear me once hear me twice thank God I'm alive
Sometimes I think too much sometimes not enough
About the ones that made you blue I sing it all the time

Call on me, and I'll be there call on me child, I'll be right here
Call me darling, you know I care, call me anytime, if you dare
Sometimes they grow up too fast sometimes not fast enough
I just mowed my lawn to smell the flowers and the grass
Sometimes life is good sometimes not so bad

Don't blame me for living the way I think I should
Sometimes life is short sometimes it's not for sure
Take a chance and look beyond the rivers and the shore

Sometimes you just should, I'd like to think I would
Sometimes you just should, stop to see the good, oh-man

Southern Girl

She walked on over and talked to me
She looked suspicious in those skinny jeans
I stood up tall and looked her in the eyes
They were as pretty as the deep blue sky

I never seen another girl like her
She was classy and tough as a tiger
I asked her questions all night long
She told me all about her favorite song

I know a thing or two about working hard and making due
It helps to have a southern girl that can wear boots or high heels
I know in the end about living life and making friends
It helps to have a southern girl with big boats and fishing reels

Nothing like Saturday in the SEC
Good friends drinks and big TVs
If my team loses, I still win
Cuz in the night we let the good times in

I like watching all the pretty girls
Rebel, Dawgs, Vols and the Gators
Cheer for me and I'll cheer for you
Kicking off in the neighborhood

I know a thing or two about working hard and making due
It helps to have a southern girl that can wear boots or high heels
I know in the end about living life and making friends
It helps to have a southern girl with big boats and fishing reels

Sweet Lovin Promises

Oh, baby I like it- Cant you see
my glow
Oh, baby you know it- I can
see it show
Oh, baby I tried it -Once or
twice before
Oh, baby I had it- Lying here
on the floor

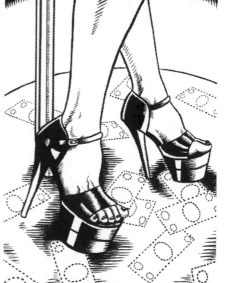

That's life on the table- That's
life on the stage
You can spend my life fortune-
But don't you forget my name

I never said I would love you
But dammit you made me say
Sweet Lovin Promises
A modern-day escapade

Oh, baby I told you- That I like it that way
Oh, baby I showed you -That I'm here to stay
Oh, baby she saw it- From not too far away
Oh, baby she touched it -Like a cat in play

Electric Avenue- Charging up my arouse
Full circuit showcase- Lighting up the dollhouse

I never said I would love you
But dammit you made me say
Sweet Lovin Promises
A modern-day escapade

Sympathy For A Rose

I was thinking about something early
this morning
An inspiration, a reputation of a
crazy man
I heard so-o many stories, I heard
so-o many lies
But I don't want to paint a weird
picture of a man that so-o many
admire
Everybody wants a shot when you
are on the top
Every day brings you hope or just
another loss

Passing by from all attempts because of your antics
Not a racist, not a feminist just a rock star poet
You carry on like a crazed apache
Stirring up some controversy
How would you feel if all your passion
Was on the path of destruction

I was thinking to myself earlier today
The intention, the fascination of a vicious game
I read so-o many articles, I seen so-o many shows
How could he think with so-o many days on the road

Outrage fuels the fire and lies ignite the spark
When they won't leave you alone

Passing by from all attempts because of your antics
Not a racist, not a sexist just a rock star poet
You carry on like a crazed apache
Stirring up some controversy
How would you feel if all your passion
Was on the path of destruction

Take Me Back

I can taste the bottom of my empty glass
See inside the darkness of my troubled past
I can smell the smoke still on my clothes
Feel the lump inside my rusty throat

Take me back where I am from to the almost heaven state
Where men were men and nouns were nouns and we all just
congregate
Take me back where I am from to the almost heaven state
Where the mountains rise and the rivers flow in a wild peaceful
place

My family keeps me humble and my feet on the ground
My friends suggest we stay late and make one more round
I met Mike and John in my twenties they threw me a rope and
pulled me in
Now the three of us are texting in our fifties and my ability to
see is wearing thin

Take me back where I am from to the almost heaven state
Where men were men and nouns were nouns and we all just
congregate
Take me back where I am from to the almost heaven state
Where the mountains rise and the rivers flow in a wild peaceful
place

Take Me Home (John Denver excerpt)

I was born in the moonshine- I grew up in the mountains
I moved down to the sunshine- To the Florida Georgia line

If I close my eyes to see- Where my heart belongs to be
Take me home- country roads- take me home

No matter where I go- No matter where I roam
The hills of West Virginia- Will always be my home

Take me home country roads- to the place where I belong
Take me home- country roads- take me home

I made friends that last forever- I worked hard to spend it on her
I know life can sometimes bite you- When you live life in the zoo

The hills and the creeks- Where my roots run so deep
Take me home- country roads- take me home

No matter where I go- No matter where I roam
The hills of West Virginia- Will always be my home

Take me home country roads- to the place where I belong
Take me home- country roads- take me home

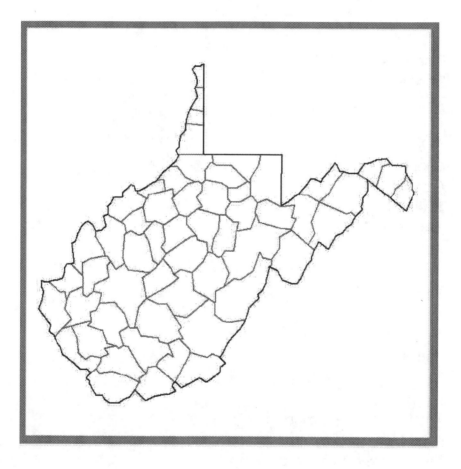

The Beast

Goodness and evil
Darkness and light
The sword cannot penetrate
The man who won't die

A jest for a jest
A smile for one's life
The sadness cannot infiltrate
The man who won't cry

The slaves have awoken their master with fear
The blood of the gods bring the face of despair

Tarred and feathered
Accused and slandered
See the wicked way

The wolf mother howls
The chase goes on
For the beast that leads astray

Caged and tortured
Abused and shattered
Hidden from the day

The wolf mother howls
The chase goes on
For the beast that leads astray

The wolf that cried boy
Learned from his mother
That lies can be deadly
And cause great disaster

The cub you once hunted
Has returned as a beast
The wolf that grew older
Has come home to feast

The slaves have awoken their master with fear
The blood of the gods bring the face of despair

Tarred and feathered
Accused and slandered
See the wicked way

The wolf mother howls
The chase goes on
For the beast that leads astray

Caged and tortured
Abused and shattered
Hidden from the day

The wolf mother howls
The chase goes on
For the beast that leads astray

The Color Of Your Eyes

I got something to dread- I feel the
pain inside my head
I feel like the walking dead- Lord, I
should have stayed in bed
The sun peels away my face- And
my pills have been misplaced
They took away my sweet grace-
Lord I don't recognize this place

I got something to say- Lord, you
got me hypnotized
I can't remember your name- But I know the color of your eyes
You know how to play the game- Lord, you know how to roll
the dice
You make me go insane- When I see the color of your eyes

Cross my heart hope to die- I will never tell you a lie
Please don't take my sunshine- Lord, you know that makes me cry
I knock before I come inside- And I wait for your reply
Like an angel she can fly- Lord, you know how to get me high

I got something to say- Lord, you got me hypnotized
I can't remember your name- But I know the color of your eyes
You know how to play the game- Lord, you know how to roll
the dice
You make me go insane- When I see the color of your eyes

The Deadly Sins Of War

If it was up to me to plant the seed, I'd bury them all alive
I'd take their tongues and misfortunes and send them all to die
Constant sorrow has gone too far they need someone to blame
False allegations and agitation are the way they play the game

Bring me peace and liberty- I want nothing more
Take a knee or take a plea- The deadly sins of war
Bring me pleasure and the treasure- I want nothing more
Take the soil or take the spoils- The deadly sins of war

The table turns and the world learns as the deadly lions play
They eat too much to enjoy their lunch a savagery display
A thousand moments on the victims' lips is the way they suck it up
So much dissension not enough attention to fill up their tea cups

Bring me peace and liberty- I want nothing more
Take a knee or take a plea- The deadly sins of war
Bring me pleasure and the treasure- I want nothing more
Take the soil or take the spoils- The deadly sins of war

If it was up to me, I'd let them bleed until they fade away
I'd spike their heads and make them beg for a deeper grave
A subtle mind fuck to the rest of us to get back where we started
They took no objection to the invasion while sleeping in their beds

The Devil Made Me Do It

Looking tall- Feeling small
Dig it up- Take it all
In the wall- Down the hall
Below the ground- The devil
crawls

Romeo and Juliet- Montague
and Capulet
Up in arms and no regrets- For
the devil made me do it

Yes, the devil, that's my excuse- No apologies for the truth
No foul no harm just empty threats- For the devil made me do it

Away we walk- Hear the talk
Drink the water- You're the pond
Break the laws- Cut your claws
Show no mercy- The devil's saw

Romeo and Juliet- Montague and Capulet
Up in arms and no regrets- For the devil made me do it

Yes, the devil, that's my excuse- No apologies for the truth
No foul no harm just empty threats- For the devil made me do it

The Gentle Wind

When I paddle-You paddle
When I stand- You Stand
When you ride the waves- You can't explain

When I walk- You walk
When I run- You run
When you beat the past- You must be fast

From coast to coast- From sea to sea
The gentle wind - A blowing breeze
From California- To Tennessee
The gentle wind- Will set you free

When we sing- You sing
When we play- You play
When the music's right- You will feel alright

When we smile- You smile
When we cry- You cry
When we hold hands- You will understand

From coast to coast- From sea to sea
The gentle wind - A blowing breeze
From California- To Tennessee
The gentle wind- Will set you free

The Highway Life

See the headlights down the road
Another town another show
Hotels and motels
Dive bars on skid row
A bottle- for my soul
A battle- for self-control

Truck stops and fistfights
Miss the kids miss the wife
Sinister and ministers
Strip clubs and white lines
We ride- into the night
Living- the highway life

Under the overpass
In between the sheets
One-night stands
And rowdy fans
Plenty of cash
Living- the highway life

Red lights and blue lights
Black shades and grey skies
Cloudy days and stormy nights
The rain- it hides the pain
Living- the highway life

The Lesbian In Me

All your problems come with the stroke of a pen- All your gripes
written down from your illusion
Never mind what the good lord gave to you- Start an angry mob
and cancel the truth

The spices in me are good enough to eat- I don't need your
pity to justify me
It's just the way I choose to spend my time- Working the crowd
on a Saturday night

The lesbian in me and the problem with you
You can't take a good lick so what do you do
The lesbian in me is a beautiful thing
I could watch her all day on the movie screen

That chip on your shoulder outweighs the facts- That egg on
your face is starting to crack
The blood on your hands shines through the black light- Since
you don't care about the facts of life

You lost control of your dignity- You lost yourself in your reality
Some say you're crazy with an attitude- But you keep moving
on without a clue

The lesbian in me and the problem with you
You cant take a good lick so what do you do
The lesbian in me is a beautiful thing
I could watch her all day on the movie screen

The Melody Rings On

Darling, you lit my heart on fire
Took me by my heart's by desire
Showed me gifts that I only could imagine

You swept in like the ocean tide
Where the rivers and sails and wind collide
Presented me with luxury and passion

The music plays from dusk til dawn
The sound of thunder beats the drum
The melody rings on and on
The pouring rain sounds like a song
The lightning crashes all night long
The melody rings on and on

My love for you is burning hot
You twist my heart into a knot
Back and forth and finally into a loop

The mare submits so gracefully
The stallion mounts like pedigree
With great power and energy from the croup

You are my sunshine
You are my lucky chime
Singing softly in the wind

You cast a shining light
Our shadow is bold and bright
The way you and I have always been

The music plays from dusk til dawn
The sound of thunder beats the drum
The melody rings on and on
The pouring rain sounds like a song
The lightning crashes all night long
The melody rings on and on

The Pain You Feel Is Real

Broken promises and empty news
Broken hearts and simple fools
Try to see what it's all about
You try so hard but your left without

Trial and error don't seem to work
Trial by law but no law clerk
Will take your case on a 2nd date
Remember the 1st time it went so great

Too many wannabees- Not enough honesty
To find your true love- To ever rise above

The pain you feel it's for real
The peace you seek it won't release
The power and strength of his grip
The happiness that you miss

You lean back, fire and pull
Shake and feel your hands so cold
But you sweat like never before
So, you get down on all fours

Reminded of pleasures that you know
Fantasize about a million more

A habit that will always last
A habit that you will regret
Too many wannabees- Not enough honesty
To find your true love- To ever rise above

The pain you feel it's for real
The peace you seek it won't release
The power and strength of his grip
The happiness that you miss

Carpet surfing on the floor
At a stranger's house behind the door
Tunnel vision tighten chest
Don't exhale choke to death

The pain you feel it's for real
The peace you seek it won't release
The power and strength of his grip
The happiness that you miss

The Poetry And Art
That Remains

As I let down my wheels and stretch out my wings
And come in for a landing so gracefully
I met someone that charmed a special piece of me
Of all the most beautiful sceneries in the world
I couldn't paint a prettier picture of a girl
Of all the oceans mountains, waterfalls, sunsets, and flowers
I couldn't imagine meeting a more perfect girl to admire
A warm pure strong creature, I trumpet her desire
She makes my nights so bright and brings color to my days
I'm gonna reserve a special place and nestle her away
She reminds me of a cool fresh water surface
With a unique saltwater side beneath
That makes her different and taste so sweet
Violets stem from her body as I kiss her gentle face
And in her eyes, I can see the poetry and art that remains
Of all the most meaningful memories I've enjoyed
I can't remember anyone that has touched me more

The Silly Things We Do

Living for tomorrow- Can't see past today
Take my bumps- Take my bruises
But I still find my way
She won't run- She won't hide
She won't run away
I bring her home another bill- I can't seem to pay

Well, the silly things that we do- When we start feeling blue
Well, the silly things that we do- To keep our spirits true
Well, the silly things that we do- When its just me and you

We bought us a camper- That we took on the road
It was small- It was loud
It was 10 years old
We kicked back and we rode hard
We saw Elvis's home
We broke down in a small hick town- Ended up getting towed

Well, the silly things that we do- When we start feeling blue
Well, the silly things that we do- To keep our spirits true
Well, the silly things that we do- When it's just me and you

The Truth

I've seen many pretty ladies in my time
Cherish all the hugs and kisses in my life
Traded all the one-night stands for a trophy wife
Just because she looks so good here by my side

Well, I been loved and I been judged
But I always tell the truth
I don't look back and I won't subtract
The things that I went thru

God oh mighty- God be true
What should I do
Truth be known- Truth be told
I'm still in love with you

I've seen many drunken ladies sit across from me
Booze, cruise, and get loose for all of us to see
I left it all behind in life for a beauty queen
Blonde hair blue eyes such a pretty scene

Well, I been loved and I been judged
But I always tell the truth
I don't look back and I won't subtract
The things that I went thru

God oh mighty - God be true
What should I do
Truth be known- Truth be told
I'm still in love with you

The World Knows Your Name

Beer- You're everything to me- You're everything I need- You keep me company
Weed- You get me high again- You're my very best friend- You help me comprehend

I fill you in my veins
You take away the pain
I see you smile- I see you grin
The world knows your name

Sex- You make me feel alive- Your grip on me is tight- You keep me satisfied
Coke- You lift me up higher- You fill my heart's desire- You warm me like a fire

I fill you in my veins
You take away the pain
I see you smile- I see you grin
The world knows your name

Dreams- You know longer have- You rip me in half- You're making me go mad
Hope- You drank your last sip- You poured out my last drip- You sunk my battleship

I fill you in my veins
You take away the pain
I see you smile- I see you grin
The world knows your name

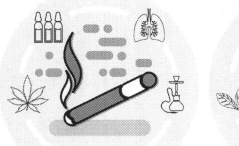

Times Like This

Well, the first thing I did when I got out of bed was to call my
very best friends
Well, the first thing I did before I went to bed was to pray for
another day- like this

We went down to the Blackwater Falls with my dog and a cooler
of beer
We sat on the hood, and we howl at the moon as we wait for
the stars to appear

My oh my what a wonderful place down by the river and lake
My oh my what a beautiful day to ride in my old Chevrolet

Times like this we reminiscence about the beauty in the sky
Times like this we reminiscence about the stories of my life

The sun shines true on the western view where the birds and
the eagles flew
A river runs thru, and the trees all grew oh the city folk don't
have a clue

I sat on a stump with my red dixie cup and the campfire kept
us safe
We hoot and we holler and broke out the Fender as the coyotes
sing and play

My oh my what a wonderful place down by the river and lake
My oh my what a beautiful day to ride in my old Chevrolet

Times like this we reminiscence about the beauty in the sky
Times like this we reminiscence about the stories of my life

Tinder Date

I met her on a tinder date- We met up at the normal place
And I bought us a whiskey and a Rolling Rock
We talked about my dragon tattoo- I leaned in and told a lie or two
Next thing I know she took her panties off

My charm goes a long-long way- It's just part of the game I play
Promise her tomorrow so I get my way today...today

Today is a good ol day- Another part of my resume
I try not to get locked down- so I can keep running around
Today is a good ol day- Another day to have my way
She goes down and I go up- I turn her around with her on top

I opened up the door for her- I recognized the bartender
He said hey haven't you been here a time or two
This place is getting way too loud- I think we should find a smaller crowd
I grabbed her hand and showed my gratitude

My charm goes a long- long way- It's just part of the game I play
Promise her tomorrow so I get what I want today...today

Today is a good ol day- Another day for a tinder date
I try so hard to get her home but I don't want to keep her long
Today is a good ol day- Another chapter another page
Tinder adds are fun to read but don't believe everything you see

Trailer Park Life

We buy our clothes from the Wal-Mart
Grab my dinner from the Quick E Mart
And we sleep around with the god dam neighbors

We hunt from our backyards
Stay up late and play cards
And fraternize with the local whores

We like having a cold one and watching hee-haw re-runs
We're living the trailer park life
We're living and dying, praying and smiling
Living the trailer park life
We're stealing and giving, sinning and grinning
Living the trailer park life

We curse yell and make crack
Smoke reds and talk smack
We been in a few bar fights

We drive trucks and Camaros
Don't worry about tomorrow
Post bail and beat up our wives

We like having a cold one and watching hee-haw re-runs
We're living the trailer park life

We're living and dying, praying and smiling
Living the trailer park life
We're stealing and giving, sinning and grinning
Living the trailer park life

We ride our bikes in the dirt
Wearing Van Halen T-shirts
Man, life has never been so good

We swim with our dogs in the pool
Never graduated from high school
Now we spend our days under the hood

We like having a cold one and watching hee-haw re-runs
We're living the trailer park life
We're living and dying, praying and smiling
Living the trailer park life
We're stealing and giving, sinning and grinning
Living the trailer park life

Unsubscribe Me

You can block me and you can unsubscribe me- I aint opening the door
I aint picking up and I don't give a fuck- I don't want you anymore

I don't need you calling me 10 times a day- I don't need to hear your voice
If you want my money you can get in line- Just like everyone else

You can block me, and you can unsubscribe me- I aint falling for your tricks
I aint giving in but I am wearing thin- I don't need nothing fixed

I don't need a car warranty and I don't want to sell my house
If you don't want to meet my attorney, then you better shut your dam mouth

I know I am not the only one that feels this way about you
You are worse than my ex-girlfriend- You are stickier than glue

I bought one thing from you before, but you never let me go
This relationship is over I have to cancel and unsubscribe below

Wait For Me

You get lost and found everyday
When I mess with your devoted heart
You get so mad and bent out of shape
Every time that I have to depart

No more worries- no more words
No more pages- no more verbs
No more sounds from my voice

Just bow your head and hum along
And wait for me all day long
Just close your eyes and tap your feet
And chase those cars in your dreams

You look me up and down and sideways
When I leave you behind for the night
It shakes you up and rattles your cage
You curl up in bed and get uptight

No more worries- no more words
No more pages- no more verbs
No more sounds from my voice

Just bow your head and hum along
And wait for me all day long
Just close your eyes and tap your feet
And chase those cars in your dreams

What's A Man To Say Or Do

I know a man named Johnny Sue
He rolled the dice all night thru
He danced a little and played the slots
Shook it up and drank a lot (Scotch)
Times were rough but he was tough
He never ever lost his touch
He sang the blues but he never cried
Even when his woman lied
About the time she ran away
With her friend he thought was gay

What's a man to say or do, when his bets begin to lose
What's a man to do or say, when his mistakes get in the way
What's a man to say or do, when his life gets the blues

I know a place just south of town
A hole in the wall never settles down
You can grab a drink at night
You can even start up a fight
I seen a few tossed down the stairs
Beat and struck with broken chairs
There is a pool table for the boys
A smokey room with 3 dart boards
If you ever get to go inside
Be sure to smile and ask Big Mike

What's a man to say or do, when his bills are way past due
What's a man to do or say, when his mistakes get in the way
What's a man to say or do, when his life gets the blues

I had a plan but it went wrong, I tried to play her favorite song
Make her proud and make her smile, But the crowd didn't like my style
So I ran for the exit door, I guess I won't go back on tour

What's a man to say or do, when his girl is getting loose
What's a man to do or say, when his mistakes get in the way
What's a man to say or do, when his life gets the blues

Whistling Dixie

Old James would be proud of his daddy's song
It took 5 years to write it -it took him way too long
He had many heartaches he broke many hearts
You can't blame the memories when you're the one at fault

You got to take your tribulations never show your hand
Just tell the dealer and make your final stand
You got to make your calculations the cards will come out right
Cash in your chips and it will be just fine

I'm just whistling dixie to my favorite song
You can play my music on and on and on
I write with a passion singing all night long
You can hear my music on and on and on

Old James wasn't feeling well he spent the night in jail
He got 10 years in Lewisburg just for selling pills
He had many nightmares he had many fights
You can't blame the system for what you do in life

You got to take your medicine, swallow your dam pride
Just tell the judge keep my ass inside
You got to face your skeletons bury it in your past
Throw away the key it will never last

I'm just whistling dixie to my favorite song
You can play my music on and on and on
I write with a passion singing all night long
You can hear my music on and on and on

Worship With Me

I'm gonna be your eyes help you see help you see- child
I'm gonna be your voice when you call on me
I'm gonna be your heart help you feel help you feel- child
I'm gonna be your back when you lean on me

I'm gonna fill your needs
I'm gonna be complete
I'm gonna pull on you
When I take the lead

I wanna pick you up
I wanna build some trust
I wanna count on you
To help me make it thru

Now come on
Can it be- lord, yes it can- child
Can it be, worship with me

I'm gonna be your ears help you hear help you hear- child
I'm gonna be the sound when you sing with me
I'm gonna be your legs help you stand help you stand- child
I'm gonna be the grace when you walk with me

I'm gonna fill your needs
I'm gonna be complete
I'm gonna pull on you
When I take the lead

I wanna pick you up
I wanna build some trust
I wanna count on you
To help me make it thru

Now come on
Can it be- lord, yes it can- child
Can it be, worship with me

You Ain't So Special

You aint so special- You're just a man
If you can't fly- No one can
You aint so special- You're just a fool
If you plagiarize- That's not cool
You aint so special- You're just a clown
If you fall in the sea- You're gonna drown

Round and round and pound for pound
You're getting old and way too loud
You think you're something but you're nothing
You aint so special anyhow

You aint so special- You're just a crook
If you rob a bank- And get off the hook
You aint so special- You're running wild
If you spill the milk- Just like a child
You aint so special- You're just disease
If you're spreading cancer- Thru the city

Round and round and pound for pound
You're getting old and way too loud
You think you're something but you're nothing
You aint so special anyhow

You got more rights- Than I have
That's not right- Take a hike

You And Me Babe

I am a wanted man
I cheat all day with my poker hand
I got keys in my pocket ready to go
I got quad aces but I play it slow

I am your worst nightmare
I follow you home in the cold night air
I am the reason that you lock the door
I know you got money in that old sock drawer

I wait all day in the shadows - I lift you up when you feel low
You fire me up when you need a light - Play with me babe and
you'll feel alright

I am a simple man
I live by the river in my mini van
I got 3 small dogs to keep me company
A mother and father that disowned me

I guard the intersections
I beg for money and my medications
I fight with my neighbor for a bag of weed
I drink my muscles and my sanity

I miss you much when you're not around - You sip and stir then you put me down
I comfort you before you fall asleep - You and me babe I am here to please

You And Me

You and me on a Friday night
Shaking our hips in the dance line
Alright ooh alright
You and I on a Saturday night
Rocking the bed in the moon light
Alright ooh alright
Walking a fine line to no where
Standing our ground so beware

Take it from me I give it to you
Anything goes whatever you do
Oh yea ooh oh yea
Time will tell if you mean well
Rose pedal flowers at the hotel
Oh yea ooh oh yea
Kick off your shoes and sit back
Lay down your head and relax

You and me on a Sunday morning
Forget the past and remember the stories
Of our lives ooh our lives
You and me thru thick and thin
Take me back to where it began
In our lives ooh our lives
Unwind the clock and tell me
Slow down the time don't hurry

Printed in the United States
by Baker & Taylor Publisher Services